The People's Hi

Shildon And District

by

Tom Hutchinson

1ST PRIZE. SHILDON RECREATION GROUND OPENING CELEBRATIONS SEPT 28TH 1912

Coat of Arms of the Urban District of Shildon. Circle enclosing three shields, two pickaxes, one hammer. Arms – Timothy Hackworth's Royal George, the Byerley Arms, the Lilburn Arms. The Byerleys and Lilburns were well-known landed gentry who owned land in the Middridge and Shildon areas, particularly in the 17th century.

Previous page: The competition winner celebrating the opening of the Recreation Ground in 1912. Who was the boy, and who was the veteran cyclist born in 1836, only 11 years after the opening of the Stockton & Darlington Railway?

Copyright © Tom Hutchinson 2003

First published in 2003 by

The People's History Ltd
Suite 1
Byron House
Seaham Grange Business Park
Seaham
Co. Durham
SR7 0PY

ISBN 1 902527 41 0

Contents

An advertisement for the Coronation celebrations of King George V and Queen Mary in 1911.

The Sidings, Shildon – 100 years ago. The biggest in the UK then, with 30 miles of track.

Men with rescue breathing apparatus, thought to be in the Shildon area. A real photographic postcard by Smithson of Shildon.

Introduction

This book looks in a visual sense at the history of Shildon and district during the 20th century, a period of great change with the decline of coal mining from the Second World War until its final demise in the 1960s, and the closure of Shildon Wagon Works in 1984. However, the book is meant to be a positive statement about the area rather than a negative one, so the vast majority of pictures of people are in happy times – at carnivals, at social events, at sport. The book is laid out in a traditional way, looking around Shildon and adjacent communities initially; then at the people through the decades. We look at the infrastructure which supported the area – the railways, coal mining and retail outlets – and finally, at Shildon Works which for 150 years employed generations of local people.

There are many photographs of people, young and old, and I have attempted to correctly name as many of them as possible. For any mistakes, I apologise. Many pictures will bring back happy memories of times past, and I hope the images will give as much pleasure to the reader as they have given to me in the compilation.

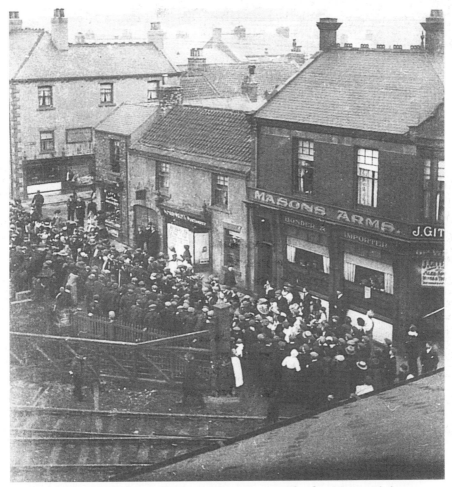

Railmen and their families at a meeting outside the Masons' Arms during the rail strike in August 1911.

Acknowledgements

I would like to thank and acknowledge all contributors for their help, pictures and information: Beamish – The North of England Open Air Museum, Timothy Hackworth Victorian & Railway Museum, Bob Abley, John Askwith, Philip Battersby, Maurice Blackett, Linda Campbell, Aubrey Clethero, Ian S. Carr, Jim Coates, George Dixon, Madge Doran, Ray Goad, Mike Grantham, Thelma Hall, Joyce Hardaker, George Hewitt, Anne Hillerby, Cliff Howe, Brian Hutchinson, Joan Johnson, Gerald Lee, George Nairn, Walter & Kathy Nunn, John Pearce, Anne Peeks, Winnie Priestley, Ray Sparks, Julia Teasdale, Norma Thompson, Tracy Tweddle, Jack Walker, Alfred & Doreen Whitlock, Mary Wright, and members of the Shildon History Recall Group, particularly Joan Ellwood and Alan Ellwood.

Selected Bibliography

Around Shildon Vera Chapman
The Darlington Saturday Half Holiday Guide W.J. Cudworth
History of the County Palatine of Durham, 1860
History of Shildon – Our Village Marjorie Lee
Shildon Coal David G. Snell
Kelly's Trade Directories, 1906, 1925, 1938
North Eastern Railway W.W. Tomlinson
First in the World – The Stockton & Darlington Railway J. Wall
Shildon – Cradle of the Railways R. Corkin
Exploring the Stockton & Darlington Railway P.W.B. Semmens
Timothy Hackworth G.E. Milburn

Shildon Junior School, 1911-12. Perfect Attendance. Back left Lizzie Yates; back 5th left Harriet Hutchinson.

THE TOWN

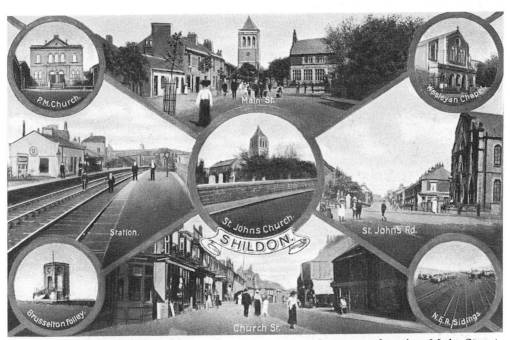

A multi-view postcard taken from St John's Church tower, showing Main Street, Church Street, St John's Road, Station and Sidings, Brusselton Folly, St John's, Wesleyan and Primitive Methodist churches. This card was sent from Blanche in Shildon to Mrs W. Johnson, 50 Queen's Road, Doncaster on 17th January 1916.

Shildon was first recorded during the Saxon period when in 821AD the estate was granted to the Church. Its name was derived from the Old English Sceld or Scyld meaning shield or refuge, and dun – a hill. In 1363 the name is given as Shyldon. The economy was a rural one run by the Lord of the Manor. In 1547 the estate known as Thickley Punchardon came into the possession of the Lilburn family. This family were anti-monarchists such that John Lilburn took part in the Northern Rebellion against Elizabeth I in 1569-70, and a later member of the family, Robert Lilburn was one of the signatories to the death warrant of Charles I. In 1717 Thickley was sold by the Lilburns. On the other hand, the Byerleys of Middridge Grange were monarchists and Anthony Byerley commanded a royal regiment in the 17th century known as 'Byerleys Bulldogs'. Both of the families are remembered in local street names.

At the beginning of the 1800s Shildon was still a hamlet of 100 inhabitants at the junction of what is now Main Street, Byerley Road and Auckland Terrace. However, small collieries were springing up in what was later called the Auckland Coalfield, and the transport of that coal to the ports of County Durham was seen as the key to the successful development of coal mining. The railway era had begun and Shildon's rise was due to being at the point where locomotive-hauled coal traffic on the Stockton & Darlington Railway was transferred from the incline worked horse-drawn wagons, and the fact that the first workshops for building and repairing locomotives and wagons were set up in the town. The population which was 115 in 1821, rose to 867 in 1831 and 2,631 in 1841 as news of the developments brought people from far and wide. Cottages were built to house these newcomers and New Shildon came into existence south of the original settlement.

Looking west along Main Street towards Shildon Lodge Colliery. On the left is the Wesleyan Church. This card was posted on 26th August 1944 from M. Robinson, Shildon to Miss Doris Worboys, Spittlesea Hospital, Luton, but the picture itself is from the 1920s.

Main Street. A postcard from the 1930s, with very little traffic. The postcard publisher is unknown, but seems to have published a series of cards of Shildon. This one being No 14.

Shildon's connection with the railways continued and expanded through the 19th century and with the opening of coal mines in the town itself from the 1850s, local prosperity was assured. By 1901, the population in Shildon was 11,759 and by 1921, 14,165. In 1925, the two separate local authorities of Shildon and Old Shildon amalgamated; with Middridge and parts of the parishes of Eldon and Redworth included in the Urban District in 1937. However, this was the time of the Great Depression when local unemployment rose to 80%. The main collieries at Adelaide, Eldon, Shildon Lodge and Shildon Colliery (Dabble Duck) closed, and the railway works made many men redundant.

What of Shildon since the Second World War? Light industrial estates were developed in the immediate post-war period, but the town was still very dependent on the old heavy industries. Deep coal mining in south west Durham completely finished in the 1960s, but the main blow to the town's economy came with the comparatively sudden closure of the railway works in 1984. In the meantime local government re-organisation meant that Shildon became part of Sedgefield District in 1974, though the town itself remains distinctive with a strong sense of community. Nowadays, major town improvement works have been completed as part of a multi-million pound strategy of regeneration which has seen a new-look town centre built, new trading estates developed, and improved roads laid out. Modern Shildon is a place for the 21st century, though extremely proud of its past.

The eastern end of Main Street, with St John's Church in the background. This early 1930s card shows the Dun Cow Hotel on the left where W. Glenn was the licensee at the time. In Kelly's 1938 Trade Directory, Andrew Crawford was in charge. The inn was renamed The Royal George at the time of the Stockton & Darlington 150th celebrations in 1975.

A late 1960s view of Main Street and St John's Church. There hadn't been many changes in the previous 30 years.

Church Street before the First World War. Note the absence of any traffic. The youngsters pose for the camera, though one girl on the right is ignoring the photographer by gazing into the Co-op window. This is still the main shopping street in Shildon, but the Co-op has relocated near the junction of Church and Primitive Streets.

Church Street. A card published by Jackson, Stationer of Church Street, and posted on 26th September 1912 from P.W. to Mr Tom Duff, 1 Jubilee Street, Toronto, Bishop Auckland. Does the cart belong to Robert Storey, Corn & Flour Dealer of Dean Street, Shildon?

A photograph of Church Street in 1966. The Co-operative Society is still in business on the right; with the shop frontage virtually unchanged in half a century. The gas lamps have been replaced by electric.

Another view of Church Street in 1966. Ahead is the Primitive Methodist Chapel built in 1868, but now demolished. On the right, next to the graveyard, is the building which was the birthplace of Bishop Auckland Co-operative Society, where the first meeting was held on 25th February 1860.

This 1930s view is along Church Street, but from east to west. The taller building on the left is Walter Willson's, grocers, at No 77. H.D. Spence was the manager there in 1938. On the right is John Robinson's hairdresser premises. This postcard is from the same publisher as the one on page 9, but No 17 in the series.

A postcard published by Christopher Smithson of Main Street, showing premises on the north side of Church Street before the First World War. The big building front right was a wine and spirit merchants run by Mrs Henry Barrasford. It is still there as a betting shop.

CHEAPSIDE, SHILDON. 20.

Above: Cheapside looking north, with the Market Place off to the right. The Black Boy branch of the Stockton & Darlington Railway originally ran parallel to Cheapside on the left, but in this 1930s view had disappeared. This card is No 20 in this Shildon series.

Left: The War Memorial was unveiled on 13th October 1923 and shows a stone plinth surmounted by a soldier. It is located in front of St John's Church and commemorates the dead of both World Wars and subsequent conflicts, from both Old and New Shildon. There is another war memorial in New Shildon that we will see later.

The Old Railway, Shildon.

This card of the 'old railway' was posted on 1st August 1920 from New Shildon to Miss Molly Holt, c/o Colonel Dawson, Westoe Village, South Shields, but the scene dates from before the First World War. The railway is the Black Boy branch of the Stockton & Darlington Railway, looking north towards the Dene Valley. Today, the houses on the left have gone, the track and telegraph poles taken up, but the trackbed still remains as a footpath from Eldon Lane to the shops in Shildon.

ALBERT STREET, SHILDON

Albert Street in about 1920, showing the King William Inn on the left corner at the junction with Cheapside. I. Reed was the licensee then, with G.W. Reed in 1925 and Isabella Reed in 1938. It's now called the New King William.

Also in Albert Street, a steamroller and water cart – machinery of a by-gone age. Note the open country behind on this eastern edge of the town about 90 years ago.

Daniel's Adamson's Coach House in the 1990s. The photograph shows the large arches through which railway coaches could be taken and housed. Daniel Adamson, landlord of the Grey Horse Inn, started a passenger service on the Stockton & Darlington Railway with a coach named 'Perseverance' in November 1827, from Shildon to Darlington. The coach house dates from 1831.

Datton (or Dattan) Gates at the junction of Main Street, New Shildon Road (later Byerley Road), Auckland Terrace and West Street (Road). This card from 1906 shows the Surtees Railway crossing the Bishop Auckland-Darlington Road on its way to Shildon Lodge (Datton), West Durham Wallsend and Copy Crooks collieries.

Shildon Lodge (Datton Gates) Crossing, looking in the opposite direction to the previous picture. Originally called Stock Lane, the road then became New Shildon Road, and nowadays Byerley Road. On the right is the Hippodrome – proper title Shildon Hippodrome & Variety Theatre.

A derelict Hippodrome, demolished in 1996. It opened as a theatre in 1911 and became a cinema a few years later. In 1922 prices for up to 1,400 patrons ranged from 3d to 8d. In the 1960s it became a bingo hall, but closed in the late '80s, and was put up for sale at £55,000. Shildon had three cinemas in 1938 – the others being Magnet (Rex) and Picture House (Essoldo).

Shildon Road, later Byerley Road, looking south. This postcard was posted on 10th February 1909 from 'Winkle Willie' in New Shildon to Miss Raine, Brusselton Farm, West Auckland. He refers to a pantomime at the Hipp, Darlington and *Robinson Crusoe* at the Eden Theatre, Bishop Auckland, and finishes his message: 'Yours to a cinder'. The Raine family still farm at Brusselton today.

New Shildon. In this postcard from 1916, we see the Society of Friends Meeting House on the left. The Society originally held meetings in private houses and then built a meeting house in Cross Street in 1862, before moving to Byerley Road in 1907.

Strand Street in 1956, just before the houses were demolished. The street developed in the middle of the 19th century as Shildon Works expanded. It is mostly open space now.

Soho Cottages originally consisted of two double-fronted houses and two cottages, one of which carries the Stockton & Darlington Railway property metal plaque G5. Timothy Hackworth lived in the right-hand house from 1831 until his death on 7th July 1850. This postcard dates from 6th August 1908 and was sent from New Shildon to Miss Louisa Cooper, 18 Red Lion Street, Redcar. On 17th July 1975 the Timothy Hackworth Victorian & Railway Museum was opened in the premises by the late Queen Mother.

Alma Road, No 10 in this Shildon series of postcards. This is a late 1930s card, but Joseph Crooks, grocer, wine & spirit merchant was in business at least from 1906 until 1938.

Hildyard Terrace, part of Redworth Road. This card from before the First World War shows the premises of Robert Lowis on the right. Mary Lowis (wife?) ran the shop between the two World Wars. The shop is still there today, but closed up. Next to it is one of a pair of the original gates from Euston Station, London which were donated to the people of Shildon in 2002 by the National Railway Museum. The other gate is sited a few yards down towards the old Masons' Arms railway crossing. The message on the back of this postcard is interesting: 'Dear Annie. Notice poor old Lizey standing out of the door and the other place is where your father works where he is at the other end of Peases Terrace. That's the bosses house and garden and ? further down?'

Redworth Road about 50 years ago. In the centre is the Railway Institute opened on this site in 1913, but originally established in Shildon by Timothy Hackworth and colleagues in 1833. The houses opposite the institute have now been demolished and replaced by the New Shildon War Memorial.

Two views of Masons' Arms crossing in 1969. It was here that Locomotion No 1 first coupled on to its train on 27th September 1825 when the Stockton & Darlington Railway opened. The inn no doubt did a roaring trade on that occasion, and was later used as a railway booking office. Opposite the pub in the top picture we see the offices of Shildon Works. In 2003, the railway and crossings have gone as well as the surrounding 19th century housing. The Masons' Arms is now called the New Masons.

More modern times. A wintry scene in Dale Road in 1991. This part of Shildon was not developed until the later part of the 19th century when Shildon Works expanded and Shildon Colliery (Dabble Duck) opened.

The park on the north side of Surtees Avenue, opened in 1912, as seen in this 1950s photograph. In the middle distance is the bandstand, opened in 1913, and nearer left, the ornate drinking fountain erected in 1914.

A close-up of the drinking fountain in 2003. The fountain itself has gone, but the canopy is shining and smart. On one of the white rounded plaques is the inscription: 'Presented to the inhabitants of Shildon by the members of the Old Shildon Workmen's Club November 1914.'

St John's Church, erected in 1833/4, was built in the Gothic style, with chancel, nave, aisles, north & south porches, and a western tower; the latter being rebuilt in 1901 at a cost of £2,000. The church itself being rebuilt and nearly doubled in size in 1881/2 to accommodate over 700 worshippers.

The interior of St John's is shown in this early 20th century postcard published by Harry Blamire who was a bookbinder, printer and stationer in Church Street. Blamires were in business in Shildon for almost the whole of the last century.

Another H. Blamire card shows St John's vicarage. This card was posted on 25th June 1910 by J.W. Denham and sent to his cousin Miss S.A. Preston, Hoyle House, Station Road, Oakworth, near Keighley. The vicar living in the premises at this time would be Rev Lilford Jervoise Causton.

All Saints Church, New Shildon, dates from 1869 when a separate parish was constituted out of the parishes of St Andrew Auckland, Heighington and Shildon (St John's). It is a stone Gothic style building, costing £3,000 and consisting of chancel, nave, north and west porches, and western tower, and could accommodate 450 worshippers. When first built, the church stood solitary on the brow of a hill and churchgoers walked through the fields to attend services. This 1980s winter view still gives a rural appearance.

Left: The Primitive Methodist Chapel was built in 1868 at the junction of Church and Primitive Streets. Behind it was also erected a Sunday School. It was one of nine Methodist churches in Old and New Shildon in 1905, though this building itself closed about 30 years ago. Timothy Hackworth and his wife, Jane, were influential in building up the Methodist cause in Shildon through giving of their time, talents and money. As an example of his preaching, Timothy had 26 appointments in the 26 weeks from November 1838.

The Wesleyan Church was opened on 8th June 1878 in Main Street. The cost was £6,000 and at the opening there was a debt of £4,150. The debt was eventually cleared, and in 1902 the church was renovated, with alterations and additions made to the organ. Prior to that in 1895 new Sunday Schools were erected in Dean Street and in 1909 Wesley Hall acquired for Adult Bible Classes. Nearly a century later, in 1973, the church was demolished. This postcard was sent from niece Carrie Snaith in Shildon on 3rd March 1910 to Mrs John Stephenson, Bleak House, Cockfield.

Occasionally new churches are built, and this one, the Methodist Church in Main Street, was built on the site of the Wesleyan Church referred to above.

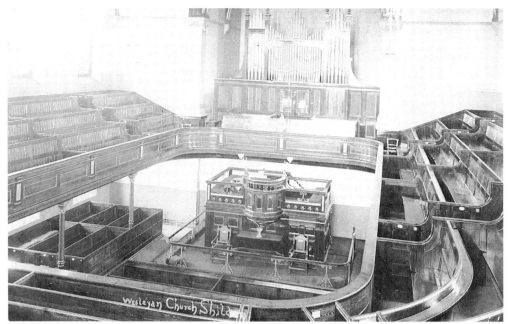

Wesleyan Church interior on a postcard from 25th April 1906. The writer 'Florrie' makes reference to 'a lovely building' in her message to Miss Easthill, 19 Scarcroft Hill, York. Note the organ and the two levels for the congregation. The Rev Robert Watkin-Jones was the minister at that time. In 1928 the church celebrated its jubilee with the publication of a souvenir programme, including a message from the minister, Edward Rees.

New Recreation Ground, 1912. The message on the back says: 'This is the photo of the recreation ground that we have got at Shildon. It is top of St John's Road. There is a new road around from Dr Fielding's to New Shildon. Now they call it the Central Parade. Don't break your jaw with the swanky names. Of course it is a great boon. The new road is not like the broken down road we had. It is wider than St John's Road and it is well rolled down too.' Another Smithson card.

N.E.R. INSTITUTE, NEW SHILDON

North Eastern Railway Institute in Redworth Road was opened in 1913, but was the third premises in which railway workers had met, originally to learn to read and write, and later for other leisure pursuits. Eighty years earlier Timothy Hackworth had put the Wesleyan schoolroom at the workers disposal, and in 1860 a new institute opened in Station Street, backed by the Stockton & Darlington Railway.

AGED MINER'S HOMES SHILDON.

Aged Miners' Homes like these at the top of Eldon Bank were built in over 70 towns and villages in County Durham. These were built in 1911 and each of the eight houses in two rows has foundation stones laid by local luminaries, such as Lady Eden, Aldermen John Wilson and A.E. Pease on 11th March.

Essoldo Cinema and Salvation Army Citadel, Station Street in 1977. The citadel was, until just before the First World War, the British School opened for 340 children in 1841 by the Stockton & Darlington Railway. The Essoldo, earlier called the Picture House, was on the site of the Mechanics Institute that had opened in 1860 with reading rooms and 2,000 books. Two years after the new institute opened in 1913 in Redworth Road, the old institute opened as a cinema. It was a rendered building of brick with an iron canopy round its corner site, and had 500 seats. Twice nightly shows were given Monday to Saturday at a charge of 4d to 1s in the 1930s. The cinema closed in about 1970 and was demolished later.

Left: Until 1925, (Old) Shildon and New Shildon were separate authorities, and thus New Shildon had its own First World War Memorial which was located in All Saints churchyard. It has been recently moved to stand opposite the Railway Institute in Redworth Road where it was re-dedicated on 10th November 2002. It commemorates the 124 men who died in that war. Those names are also inscribed on the war memorial in front of St John's Church.

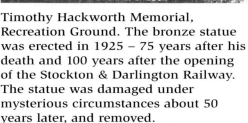

Timothy Hackworth Memorial, Recreation Ground. The bronze statue was erected in 1925 – 75 years after his death and 100 years after the opening of the Stockton & Darlington Railway. The statue was damaged under mysterious circumstances about 50 years later, and removed.

A new statue of Timothy Hackworth has been erected on the same site, as this photograph from 2003 shows. It seems stockier around the waist and shoulders compared to the original, but is pleasing.

Timothy Hackworth, 1786-1850. His association with Shildon began in 1825 when he arrived in the town 'to have superintendence of the permanent and locomotive engines' on the Stockton & Darlington Railway. Timothy started as an apprentice at Wylam Colliery and eventually succeeded his father there as foreman blacksmith. He seemingly played some part in the building of William Hedley's locomotives 'Wylam Dilly' and 'Puffing Billy' in 1813-15, and after he went to Walbottle Colliery in 1817, he cemented his status as a gifted engineer by designing static engines. In 1824 Timothy took up an invitation to temporarily manage the Forth Street Works, Newcastle, of Robert Stephenson & Co. This included the supervision of locomotive construction, including the building of 'Locomotion' for the fledging Stockton & Darlington Railway. He returned to Walbottle for a few months, but handed in his notice at the pit in early 1825. The next step was the job offer from the Stockton & Darlington where his technical expertise and skills in man-management laid the foundation of the outstanding work at Shildon. The second part of his working life was from 1825 to 1850. During that period he built numerous locomotives, initially working for the Stockton & Darlington and from 1833 contracting with the company to work traffic and maintain locomotives. That contractual arrangement allowed him to work professionally on a private basis which he did full-time from 1840 when he severed direct links with the railway company. For the next ten years he manufactured locomotives for an international as well as British market.

Another multi-view card of Shildon showing Main Street, All Saints Church, Fountain in the Park, and Council Schools, Byerley Road. The photographs probably date from the late 1940s.

We'll end this section with a modern photograph of very recent developments in 1998 in Church Street, with the arches and friezes where once 19th century shops stood, and where a regular market now takes place. Off to the left is a second statue of Timothy Hackworth silhouetted under the canopy. Why should an individual have two statues in a small town? Maybe an extract from his obituary explains why: 'He was a man of ingenious and active mind; kind and liberal in disposition; plain and unassuming in his manners; cheerful and edifying in his conversation; of deep and fervent piety and untiring in his endeavours to promote the well-being of his fellow creatures.'

THE VILLAGES

Heighington – view south west from the church tower of the green surrounded by houses. The village pump is in the foreground adjacent to the bus stop. This postcard probably dates from the 1950s.

Heighington is situated about 500 feet above sea level, with fine views south towards Darlington and the Tees valley. The *Darlington Saturday Holiday Guide* of 1882 says: 'the village, with its large green round which it is built, its quaint pump, its few old fashioned houses, and its bright gardens, is a pleasant one.' It is an ancient village, having a church here for over 850 years – since before the Conquest says Kelly's Directory of 1906. In the Boldon Book of 1183 the village had 16 villeins and five cottagers. Fortunately, from an environmental point of view, the village is about three miles beyond the southern boundary of the Durham coalfield and so it has remained a rural settlement. The coming of the railway did not permanently affect the village even though the population increased from 557 in 1821 to 767 in 1831; by 1841 it had dropped to 695 and by 1901 it was only 652. By 1931 it had reached 919. The railway station is over one mile to the east, and was originally called Aycliffe Lane in 1825 when Locomotion No 1 made its first journey from Shildon to Stockton. The village has a bypass road today, so is much safer and quieter than years ago. New housing has been built, particularly west of the green, and there seems to be a high level of community spirit around as seen in the Millennium celebrations and others since.

A 1930s card No 3 published by Geoff Prudhoe, Darlington, of the houses along the north side of the green. In the middle of the row is the grocery shop of Fred Sowerby. It is still a shop today.

Another Geoff Prudhoe card showing the green looking east. A tranquil scene from between the two World Wars of the horses grazing near the pond. Behind the horses is the former village hall that was in use until the mid 1960s.

The green looking north. Another postcard from the 1950s. The white building on the left is the Bay Horse public house. A lady called Ann Sophia Bowser was the licensee at the Bay Horse for at least 32 years from 1906 to 1938. Behind the figure is the disused water pant (pump). There is a Rural District Council notice attached to it which says: 'Persons riding or driving cattle on the footpaths will be prosecuted.'

This is an earlier view of the south end of the green, dating from 3rd February 1911 when it was sent from Gran in Heighington to Miss Ruth Johnson, Milburn Street, Crook. The pond was at the low part of the green and fed by surplus water from the village pump higher up the bank. Its stone rim can be clearly seen on the right. One of the houses along the bottom of the green is called Pond House. The shop on the right may have been a butcher's, possibly James Davison's.

A more modern, early 1960s postcard showing St Michael's Church and the old school which was opened in 1812 and enlarged in 1831. The school became the new village hall after 1965. The tall building off to the left past the white houses is the Methodist Chapel opened in 1872. This card was published by the I'Anson family who ran the post office from at least the 1920s until the 1980s. Unfortunately, at the time of writing the post office is closed.

The War Memorial sited in front of St Michael's Church in this postcard published by Nellie Best, grocer in the village in the 1920s. There are 17 names inscribed on the two First World War plaques and ten more names from the Second World War on the plinth at the bottom of the cross.

This card is dated 8th September 1915 and shows the inside of St Michael's Church. Much of the church is visibly Norman, including the chancel, tower with its narrow windows and the south

doorway, which was originally on the north side of the building. Excavations in 1981 though, produced evidence of 10th century foundations under the chancel and nave. The tower has a 15th century parapet with gargoyles at the corners and the oak pulpit dates from 1530. The church was restored in 1873 at a cost of £3,709.

A long distance view of Redworth from the north. This card which was posted from New Shildon on 23rd July 1906 to Miss E. Bell, 40 King Street, Shotton Colliery, has the following message: 'Dear Lizzy. I write these few lines to let you know that (I) have been moved about a week ago. And Mother is down at J. Dowson butcher and brought another little boy for them. And we are thinking of going to Penrith next Saturday for a day or two to keep the heart up as little Willie will be coming soon. No 6 Diamond St. New Shildon. xxxx for Baby, W.J.' Joseph Dowson had a shop in Alma Road, Shildon. James Beddison, the publisher of this card, was a hairdresser and tobacconist in New Shildon.

A closer look at Redworth, mentioned in the Boldon Book in 1123. The village developed in parallel with the adjacent mansion of Redworth Hall, both owned by the Surtees family until 1952. An idyllic scene looking down Mill Lane over 90 years ago.

Redworth Hall – the upper card is a Smithson of Shildon view showing the hall before the First World War when it was owned by Henry Siward Balliol Surtees. The hall had been bought by Robert Surtees in 1744 and rebuilt by him. His grandson Henry built the Great Hall in 1860, and the estate title changed from Redworth House to Redworth Hall. Henry Siward sold the property to Durham County Council in 1952 for tax reasons, and it became a residential school. Nowadays (*below*) it is a hotel and conference centre.

At Brusselton, at a height of 700 feet, was a folly. This tower was built for observation purposes by the Carr family in the 18th century. On a clear day, Penshaw Monument, Durham Cathedral and the cliffs at Saltburn could be seen. Eventually, the folly became derelict, the iron railings were taken – possibly for the Second World War effort – and it was demolished over 50 years ago. This postcard of 6th July 1911 from H at New Shildon was sent to Mrs Flamson, 6 Prospect Terrace, Annfield Plain, and shows the folly in reasonable condition.

The following three photographs show the houses at Brusselton incline summit in 1966 and '67. The Stockton & Darlington Railway winding engine here hauled loaded coal wagons up from West Auckland and let them down eastwards to Shildon where steam locomotives took over. The track ran through the cutting below the houses in North Terrace.

North Terrace facing west. The building on the left is the old engine house.

North Terrace facing east. These houses were built by the railway company to house its workers on the incline. They've been demolished.

South Terrace on the right, facing east. Part of South Terrace is still there today, as is the engineman's house and engine house sticking out behind.

Middridge east end, showing the Masons' Arms in the early years of the last century. In Kelly's 1906 trade directory, John Timms was listed as the licensee; in 1925, James Briggs; in 1938, John Dobson. Today, where the pub was is an open space. All the postcards of Middridge bar the one at the bottom of page 45, were published as a set by H. Coates, 70 High Street, Willington.

Middridge is mentioned in the Boldon Book of 1183. Then there were fifteen villeins and four cottagers in Middridge who rendered for their lands the usual contributions of grain, wood, hens, and other payments in kind and money, besides customary labour. According to Kelly's Directory of 1906, Middridge was a place which 'in the 17th century and later was commonly believed to be the haunt of innumerable fairies, and the local folk-lore preserves curious and detailed traditions of their gatherings round a lofty hill near the village, and the strange adventures of villagers who ventured near it.' However, more factual information says that the village only increased in population by 100 to 300 between 1801 and 1851, and they lived in 60 houses. In 1851 there were two public houses, a school and a Wesleyan chapel. Eventually though, coal mining spread eastwards from Shildon, and Eden pit was opened in about 1880. The population increased to 774 by 1901 and 36 houses were built next to the pit. The mining effect was comparatively short-lived on the village compared to elsewhere in County Durham in that by 1921 the population was 72 less than 20 years earlier and mining had been suspended at the local pit. The opening of a drift mine in the 1950s didn't effect the nature of the village as it was half a mile away. Today, many of the residents commute to jobs in the adjacent towns, and do their shopping there as there are no shops in the village. The urban sprawl of Newton Aycliffe has been kept on the other side of Tuft Hill, so Middridge, hopefully, retains some of the character of the days of fairies and folk-lore.

Middridge School in about 1915. The building dates from 1817. It was enlarged in 1892, at a cost of £300, to accomodate 200 children. During its early years it was also used for Sunday worship until Shildon parish was constituted in 1837. William White was the headmaster before the First World War, and Charles Pearce in 1925. The building is now the village hall.

To the left of the telegraph post is the Bay Horse pub on the south side of the village green. William Hull was the first recorded licensee in 1828 though the building itself is probably 18th century. This postcard dates from the 1920s when Mrs Mary Dove was the licensee, followed by Edward Newton in 1929.

George Butterfield's butcher's shop and van on the north side of the green in about 1930. Butterfield's traded as butchers through the first half of the 20th century. Behind the shop was an abattoir. The people in the picture are here posed for Mr Coates, the photographer.

In the centre is the Primitive Methodist Chapel opened in 1884 and behind it the pit heap from Middridge Colliery. Services at the chapel ceased in 1941, and the chapel and two adjacent cottages sold in 1957. The chapel stone was later used to build a bungalow. The shop on the right was the post office run by John Robson. On the left is J.W. Butterfield's butcher's shop.

North side in the late 1920s. In the middle behind the single-storey cottage is the winding gear of Middridge Colliery.

A much later picture than the bottom one on page 43. The Bay Horse has been renovated in this 1960s view. Today it has been done up again and is called the Poacher's Pocket; the only pub in the village where once there were three – the third one being the King's Arms which closed in the 1930s, though there had been another in existence in the 19th century called the Shoulder of Mutton – when the only other competition was the Bay Horse.

The entrance to Middridge from Shildon; the road being straddled by the mineral railway line from Middridge Colliery which went one mile down to the Darlington-Bishop Auckland branch line east of Shildon. The spectators are posed again for the camera, but the main objective of the photographer was the bridge. The bridge has long gone, but there is a public footpath along the trackbed today.

Charles Pit and Colliery Row, showing the chimney and winding gear. The pit was part of the Middridge Colliery complex which also included Eden Pit. Mining was started in about 1880 by the Weardale Iron & Coal Co Ltd and household and manufacturing coal was produced. The colliery was in its heyday in about 1896 when 432 men worked there under the management of Richard Elves. However, by 1914 coal production had been suspended and only four men were employed. In 1954, the National Coal Board opened Middridge Drift half-mile to the north west of the deep mine and, in 1960, 354 men were employed, though by 1966 it had been closed. In 1988 it re-opened as a private licensed mine. Mining has ceased now. This 1920s card was sent from Nora in Middridge to Miss Ada Butterfield, Sydenham Road, Belle Vue, West Hartlepool.

Old Eldon. The manor of Eldon is first mentioned in a charter of King Canute, who gave it to the shrine of St Cuthbert at Durham in 1020 when he came on a pilgrimage. The manor was acquired in 1792 by Sir John Scott of Newcastle, then Solicitor-General, who became Lord Chancellor in 1802. In 1821 he was created Earl of Eldon. At 500 feet in altitude, Old Eldon has always remained rural in character whereas Eldon, 150 feet lower, was part of the Auckland Coalfield development in the 19th century and until recently the site of open-cast coal mining. The Methodist chapel shown in this 90-year-old card was opened in 1893, and demolished long ago, so that no sign of its existence remains now.

St Mark's Church, Eldon, was consecrated on 22nd July 1879 by Dr Lightfoot, Bishop of Durham. It was built at a cost of £3,436 to serve the fast growing coal mining population of the Dene Valley, which reached 3,418 in number in 1881. This postcard was sent from Harold to Reg Eves, High Street, Coatham, Redcar on 8th February 1915. He mentions buying a new pair of brown boots for 5/6; normal price 15/6!

Left: The vicarage at Eldon. The first vicar was William Noble. At the time of this card, 1910, Charles John Gray was the vicar. The life of the church was at its peak in his time there, with a huge Sunday School of 40 teachers, and a choir 60 strong. Priests-in-charge have served the parish since 1959.

Below: A Smithson of Shildon postcard showing the interior of St Mark's Church. Is the man on the left one of the churchwardens, George Thorpe or Robert Peverell? This postcard was sent by Sallie, 4 Spencer Street, Eldon Lane on 20th June 1912 to Miss O. Sanderson, Prospect Cottage, Redcar.

Eldon – the church hall opened in 1912 at a cost of £1,500. The hall is still there, but converted into flats.

John Daniel Race's post office at the junction of Spencer Street and Deanery Street, Eldon Lane. The window and wall advertisements include Quaker Oats, Zebra Shoe Polish and Glendennis Beef & Malt is Best. The children were always keen to be in the picture nearly 100 years ago.

Two more commercial premises in High Street, Eldon Lane, about 95 years ago; South Durham Inn, licensee George Emmerson; and Richard Dixon, painter. Richard Dixon later became the postmaster, and his old premises still houses the post office. The pub is now a one-stop shop.

Left: Spencer Street, Eldon Lane, in 1970. The Club Cinema opened in about 1927 and was run by the local workingmen's club, though it had a manager, George Harwood, for many years. It seated 668 people and there were often three changes of programme weekly, and a separate Sunday show. Prices in 1956 were 9d to 1s 6d. Films ceased not long after this photograph was taken. It is still part of the club premises – the club's centenary is in 2009.

PEOPLE

All Saints Young Men's Bible Class Football Team, 1920-21. An 80-year-old photograph showing a team who played the most popular sport in this country. This Smithson of Shildon postcard is one of the last that he published in the town before leaving to take over the post office in West Witton, Wensleydale.

A team from Heighington in 1925 – Heighington Ramblers. Back, left to right: Harry Hogg, Billy Searle, Albert Metcalfe, George Brown, unknown, unknown, Ernie Robinson, Tommy Thompson. Front: unknown, Jimmy Mansfield, unknown, unknown, Jimmy Robinson, unknown.

SHILDON FOOTBALL CLUB

Shildon FC, 1936. An Ardath Tobacco Co cigarette card showing the team who won the Northern League Championship four years running from 1933-34, and League Cup in 1933-34 and '34-35. Back, left to right: G. Charlton, G. Veitch, S. Smith, G. Hope, F. Mason, F. Oliver, J. Davison. Front: W. Walker, A. Wild, H. Nicholson (captain), D. Plank, O. McGinn.

Heighington FC Juniors in 1935-36. Back, left to right: J. Scofield, K. Clapham, A. Bussey, A. Walker, T. Hindmarsh, B. Gedling, H. Gathwaite, C. Kane, P. Wearmouth, J. Clapham, M. Green. Middle: M. Thornton. Front: J. Carnan, H. Blades, B. Ingledew, D. Whitehead (captain), unknown. Winners of the Darlington Junior Cup and South Durham Divisional Cup.

Shildon Works Welders Team, 1949. Back, left to right: Billy Potter, Tommy Stubbs, John Brown, Arnie Milburn, Harold Close, George Alderson, Nat Clarkson. Front: G. Metcalfe, John Gardener, E. Coatsworth, Tommy Bradley, Chubby Dent, J. Howe. Mascot: Ray Sparks.

Shildon All Saints Rovers FC, 1953-54, of Darlington Church & Friendly League. Back, left to right: Ralph Howe, Eric Brass, Ossy Hill, Eric Ewbank, Alan Welch, Bill Shaw, Saxroma Noble, Brian Hogg. Front: Donald Ketley, Bryan Ellison, Bill Raine, Dennis Merryweather, Dennis Hughf.

Shildon Works FC, late 1950s. Back, left to right: Albert Robinson, Matty Brownless, Reg Woods, Tom Lowery, Ossie Walsh, Robin Chisholm, John Siddle. Front: Graham Gordon, Wilf Robinson, John Wilde, Allan Welsh, Laurie Lithgoe.

A Coates of Willington postcard from about 1921 showing Middridge Cricket Club. Back left in tie is Charles Gibbeson. Front, 3rd left, David Wheldon; 5th left is Tommy Harker. Note the old railway guards' van used as a score box.

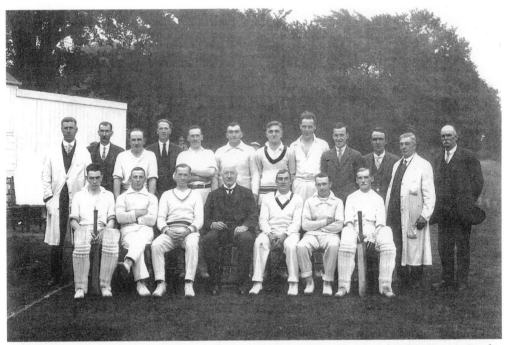

A more modern team, but still 67 years ago in 1936. Shildon LNER Team. Back, left to right: 2nd George Saunders, 3rd Ralph Emmerson. Front, first four from left: Thomas Saunders, James Mitchell, Charles Stephenson, Wells Hood (Works Manager). Others in the photo include: Billy Oliver, Harold Childs, Fred & Stan Borrowdale, Billy Romaine and Billy Baxter.

Shildon Town
Cricket Club,
1972. Back:
W. Dodshon,
P. Davison,
N. Spottiswood,
C. Dains,
S. Wallice.
Front:
D. Hancock,
G. Henderson
(captain),
D. Scott,
J. Pearce,
N. Nash,
A. Dixon. The
1970s hair
styles were
always so
distinctive!

Now, to indoor sports. Shildon Snooker & Billiards Team sometime in the 1950s. Back, left to right: Bartie Morland, Sid Ingledew, Archie Harwood, Harry Johnson. Middle: Dick Calvert, Tommy Taylor, unknown, Ernie Gibbon, Bob Aire, Anty Collins, ? Harewood, Alf Baxter, George Nixon. Front: Ned Hammond, Bob Sproats, Jimmy Bennett, Chas Denham. Certainly a successful team.

Sport of a different sort. Shildon Athletic Weightlifting Club, 1949. The people include: K. Beatham, P. Dudas, K. Hall, D. Holmes, D. Kell, R. Raine, J. Smith, T. Storey, A. Whitlock, D. White and sister, ? Bowes, ? Walton. Alf Ketley was the instructor.

Shildon British Rail Boxing Club, 1955. Back, left to right: John Dunn, Will Appleby, Bryan White, John Walton, Peter German, Tommy Jacques (trainer). Middle: unknown, Raymond Clarkson, unknown, Colin Raine, unknown. Front: George Giles, unknown, Wilf Fieldson, unknown.

PERFECT ATTENDANCE. 1911-12.

Now to education over a period of 85 years. A Smithson postcard from 1911-12 of Perfect Attendance at the Council School. The teacher was J. Wright. Front, 2nd left, with left elbow on desk is Harry Thirkell; 4th left, right elbow raised, his brother Teddy.

A woodwork class in about 1915. Note the regimentation of the boys, though the room hasn't been cleaned up for the photographer. John Hutchinson is probably in the picture. Unfortunately, no one else has been identified as yet.

The National School in Church Street, about 1914. In the picture: 1st left Jean Murray; 4th left Lizzie Yates; 7th left (front) Harriet Hutchinson (who later married Harry Thirkell who's in the picture opposite).

Another class in the same school – infants though – two years later. These school buildings eventually became the local scouts hall. Front row behind sign C256, left to right: Sally Walker, Jenny Chandler, Bella English. Second row, 2nd right: Lily Airey. Fourth row, 2nd right: Bertha Lewis, 3rd right was Edgar Ayre. Teacher, back left: Miss Richardson.

Shildon Council Schools, Form I, November 1922. Back, left to right: Doris Hutchinson, Bella English, Jane Metcalfe, Isobel Elliot, Eva Ayre, Edith Williamson, Millie Landick. Middle: Lizzie Peacock, Florie Bloomer, Edith Bloomfield, Winnie Charlton, Nellie Jackson, Evelyn Williamson, Miss Coates. Front: Jenny Tarn, Bella Topham, Minnie Graydon, Mary Yates, Nan Elliot, Jenny Coxon, Connie Rymer, Jenny Chandler. Jane Metcalfe taught from 1931 to 1971 at St Anne's C. of E. Infants & Junior School, Bishop Auckland. She was a good teacher.

Shildon Council School, 1951. Back, left to right: B. Barnes, D. Leeman, J. Giles, W. Reece. Middle: J. Flatman, S. Ramsay, J. Atkinson, D. Tutin, P. Blamire, N. Simpson, A. Taylor, J. Lawrence, R. Stephenson. Front: P. Horan, W. Townsend, N. Petty, J. Tully, R. Purdham, K. Lishman, J. Wilson, W. Storey, R. Goad.

Timothy Hackworth School, Class 6, 1968-69. Back, left to right: Lynn Stephenson, Gillian Wade, Stephen Mawson, unknown, Tony Marshall, Stephen Stabler, Michael Bird. Front: Jeffrey Sharp, Julia Moore, Tony Hutchinson, unknown, Sharon Mawson, Arthur Thompson.

Timothy Hackworth Recorder Group, 1968-69. Back, left to right: Christine Bailey, Claire Pickering, Janet Wilkinson, unknown. Front: Anne Richardson, Sandra Waller, Catherine O'Neil, Julia Hutchinson, Gillian Wade.

Sunnydale School, Year 11D, 1995. Back row, left to right: Richard Baxter, Mark Schact, Steven McTearnan, Ryan Ainsworth, Gary Morrison, Simon Smith, Christopher Peacock, David Penfold. Middle: Andrew Lee, Cathleen Buckley, Michael Hickford, Christopher Scott, Shaun Dent, Michael Parsley, Michelle Stocks, Charlene Whensley, Stephen Thompson. Front: Stacy Earle, Janine Thompson, Diane Merchant, Emma Boulton, Michelle Race, Sarah Briddick, Sarah Weldon, Stacey Gallagher, Nicola Mundy.

Sunnydale School, Year 11D, 1996. Back row, left to right: Stuart Bainbridge, Paul Readman, Luke Roe, Leigh Thompson, Kris Coley, Jonathan Coates, Paul Baynham, Adrian Ingledew. Middle: Lisa Houghton, Glen Archer, Charles Tindale, Robert Lee, Stuart Ridley, Lee Blackett, Christopher Danson, Susan Nicholson. Front: Kimberley Scaife, Tina Everitt, Samantha Bayles, Elizabeth Bird, H. Moore (teacher), Alexandra Caygill, Hayley Read, Hayley Thompson, Danielle Thompson.

What about festivities and commemorations? Shildon Endeavour Minstrels, 1904-5. The message on the reverse, dated 30th October 1905 says: 'Dear Annie. Hope you like this one. There are some good looking young men on this card. This is all at present. From your Mother.' (The full name and address has, unfortunately, been scrubbed out.)

Shildon Show, 1905. Has the event finished? The big crowd wait in anticipation. The show covered horticulture, industrial, fine arts and lady amateur sections, classes for horse leaping, poultry, pigeons, rabbits, cats and cavies.

Shildon Show, 1907. The military presence was significant in those early days. The 18th Hussars at play. Military tournaments and concerts were regular features, along with sports events.

The next year, 1908, was the turn of the Seaforth Highlanders with their gymnastic team. This Smithson card was sent on 1st September 1908 to Miss M. Elliot, Brown Knowe, Bellingham, Northumberland.

Coronation celebrations of George V and Queen Mary, 1911. The band and procession at the bottom of Auckland Terrace, Shildon. A postcard sent to Mrs E. Hutton, Hareshaw Head, Bellingham, from Shildon.

Further 1911 Coronation festivities in Main Street, Shildon. The horse decked out with the 'Royal' motif. Prizes of 10/-, 5/- and 2/6 were offered by Shildon Urban District Council for the best decorated business premises and houses – rateable value under £10 and value £10 and over – on the route of the procession.

The same Coronation, but at Eldon. The scouts marching behind the carts. The Coronation itself was on 22nd June 1911.

Eldon again. There seems to be some sort of pageant going on. The publisher of these cards looks as though he did a series. This card is No 1; the previous card No 4.

The next year, 1912, we have a procession down Byerley Road, Shildon, going to the opening of the Recreation Ground on 26th September. The two girls in front in the white are, from left, Ada Ruddham and Ethel Hodgson.

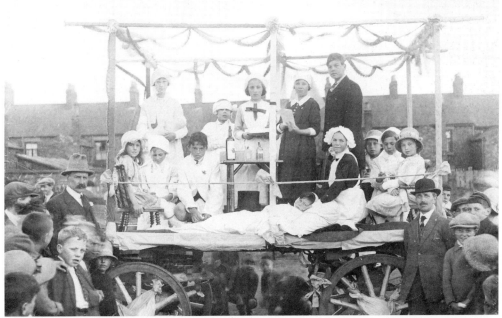

Middridge Carnival, 1926. On the float, back, left to right: Violet Lumsden, Jackie Dodds, Edith Sedgewick, Nancy Farnaby, Jim Bennett. Front on float: Irene Warminger, Louise Robinson, Jackie Penman, Sydney Wheldon, Doris Wheldon, Elsie Todd, Margaret Dodds, Sybil Ruecroft. Man on left in hat: Mr Bennett; on right in hat: Mr Ruecroft.

The next three cards celebrate the ending of the Second World War, with street parties in New Shildon. First, Beresford Street, with as many names as possible: Mesdames: Bibby, Burns, Emmerson, Hampton, Lawson, Ranson, Stott, Whitlock; Mrs Charlton & family, Mrs Doran & family, Mrs Horan & family; Mr & Mrs Baxter & family, Mr Robson & family, Mr & Mrs Elders, Mr & Mrs Hughf; Mary Alderson, Jennie Cousins, Brenda Hampton, Joan Jackson, Barbara Lee, Julia Murphy, Lucy Paylor; Christine Handley & sister; Ena Thornton & mother, sister & daughter; Joyce & John Lumsden & Jimmy; Robert (Bobby) Horner & mother; Wilf Bowe, Jacky Gibbon, Gordon Hampton, Dick James, John Merryweather, Neil Petty, Billy Proud, John Stainthorpe. Other names Haw and Johnson.

Bouch Street. Included are: Mesdames Clethero, Dickinson, Parkin, Young; Mrs Bell & Nora, Mrs Beard & Catherine, Mrs Fagan & Derek, Mrs Townsend & children; Mr & Mrs Foster, Mr & Mrs Kell, Mr & Mrs Reed & Alma, Mr & Mrs Wade & children, Sarah Emmerson. Other names Ainscough and Robinson.

Kilburn Street. Back and third rows included: George Crawford, Maud Barry, Terry Atkinson, Rene Haw, Freda Hanley, Hilda Haw, Billy Tarn, Una Wilson, Greta Wilson, Jenny Brown, Beatie Marshall, Maggie Bennett, Stephen Leng, and Mesdames Anderson, Bowser, Haw, Hutchinson, Jackson, Leng, Robinson, Strong, Wilson. Second row standing included: Marina Haw, Neil Richmond, Billy Strong, Derek Baker, Edith Scott, Margaret Proud, Edith Tweddle, Betty Burnett, Dorothy Barrie, Joyce Scott, Willy Scott, Norma Jackson, John Elgey, Allan Rutter, Christine Catchpole, Colin Tarn, Joan Jackson. Front row, kneeling or sitting included: Neil Hankey, Marjorie Ankers, Timothy Clarkson, Dennis Elgey, Roger Clarkson, Colin Hanley, John Atkinson, Penelope Clarkson, Sylvia Robinson, Dorothy Longmire, Kathleen Haw, Lynn Hutchinson, Joan Bennett, Kenneth Tweddle, Ian Hutchinson, Brian Hogg, Brian Bullyment.

All Saints Coronation Festivities, 1953, held on the vicarage lawn. Back row, left to right: Christine Calvert, Margaret Hardy, Rita White, Janice Debenham, Penelope Clarkson. Front: Beryl Debenham, Jennifer Hall, Joan Collins, Avril Palmerley, Ann Brownson. Queen: Ida White.

All Saints Day Tea, 1953. The participants included: Hartley Appleby, Maureen Bellis, Keith & Judith Ebbage, Christine Handley, Marion Johnson, Stanley Pattinson, Kenneth Tweddle, George Watcham, Jeffrey Watson, Donald Webb, Kathleen Welford, Walter & Mrs I. Brownson, Harry & Mrs H. Johnson, Mesdames Hodgson, Lumsden, Robinson and M. Robinson, and Miss Cousins.

Shildon Scouts Carnival on 11th June 1959. Note how types of entertainment have changed in the first half of the 20th century.

Right: Jazz bands became the vogue from the 1960s. This one is in Church Street, Shildon in 1963.

Below: Now back in time again to more serious musical matters – a choir. A Smithson postcard showing Shildon Male Voice Choir in 1912.

All Saints Church Choir, 1927. Back row, left to right included: Gordon Harwood, Norman Atkinson, Wilf Bowe, Joe Leng, Syd Ebbage, W. Marshall and ? Micklethwaite. Second row included: Ted Minto (organist), Linda Hodgson, W. Leng, Mr Minto (choirmaster). Front row included: Bill Gray, Bobby Cousins, John Kershaw, Rev Shaddick, Ernest Thompson, Bill Harwood. Front sitting, 2nd left: Lenny Beard.

The Shildon Youth Choir in 1948 pictured in Dr Anderson's garden. The choir performed light music in the 1940s and early '50s, and appeared on BBC Radio Home Service broadcasts from Newcastle. Back, left to right: J. Smith, B. Calvert, unknown, R. Studham, unknown, G. Romaine, J. Dowson, W. Conlan, ? Littlefair, A. Bowron, N. Richmond, F. Pickering, J. Tomlin, D. Wetherell. Third row: W. Johnson, A. Richardson, D. Wigington; then the ladies: S. Shaw, D. Coates, D. Kitching, R. Mitchell, A. Murray, D. Linsey, J. Thompson, E. Sowerby, unknown, C. Bryant, J. Linsey, M. Spenceley. Second row: L. Ayre, E. Kasher, P. Luther, O. Caygill, J. Robinson, G. Dowson, F. Murray, J. Sweet, B. Eales, M. Patterson, M. Moody, G. Johnson, V. Nicklin, A. Reed, J. Robinson, M. Thirkell. Front: M. Wright, M. Thwaites, M. Hobbs, R. Jeffries, M. Pattinson, D. Parker, D. Richardson, Harold & Zilpha Pletts (leader and founder respectively), daughter Connie Pletts, J. Jackson, E. West, G. Carlin, unknown, M. Metcalf.

Shildon Youth Choir and Hackworth Singers at the Railway Institute, 24th November 1955 – disbanding party after the death of Harold Pletts and his daughter Connie's move out of the town. Back, left to right: E. Pearson, E. Blenkin, M. Mallam, A. Overend, E. Kasher, R. Wigington, unknown, A. Richardson, J. Mason, R. Goad. Fourth row: K. Strophair, E. Grainger, A. Charlton, M. Alderson, J. Reynolds, A. Reynolds, E. Rayner, G. Morris, unknown, E. Forbes. Third row: D. Hughf, B. Davidson, D. Richardson, O. Rutherford, A. Welch, N. Jackson, K. Lowe, V. Johnson, R. Holdsworth, B. West, R. Dixon. Second row: A. Collins, B. Storey, K. Taylor, A. Hawkins, J. Pletts, N. Richardson, J. Ketley, G. Lee, D. Wigington. Front: G. Dowson, unknown, E. West, N. Bailey, D. Ellenor, J. Jackson, R. McConnell.

Members of Church Street Methodist Operatic Group who presented the opera 'Les Cloche De Cornville' in November 1948. Back row, left to right: T. I'Anson, D. Trudgill, A. Richardson, G. Harvey, R. Goad, G. Stephenson, W. Metcalfe, G. Webb, J. Bywell, A. Robson, J. Tomlin, T. Crooks, J. Stannard. Third row, women: M. Spensley, D. Brunskill, A. Walker, M. Yates, J. Forbes, M. Wright, J. Thompson. Second row: D. Baker, N. Gladwin, A. Barras, W. Trudgill, N. Samms, L. Samms, J. Robinson, M. Thwaites, J. Thwaites, J. Scales, D. Pearce, I. Pearce, R. Forbes, C. Lewis. Front row: G. Johnson, C. I'Anson, A. Richardson, J. Stephenson, J. Guy, V. Vickers, ? Chapman, J. Stephenson, H. Peverley, A. Barras, F. Johnson, T. Peart, Z. Pletts, E. Trudgill.

Now listen to the band. New Shildon Temperance Silver Band, 1906-7. Back, left to right: F. Tarn, G. Longstaff, H. Place, W. Barras, C.E. Stephenson, J. Bellis, T. Bellis, F. Burgess, H. Pearce. Middle: E. Nicholson, R. Butterfield, J. White, F. Best, O. Hann, J. Scott, H. Gibbon, I. Chaplin, T. Collinson, T. Longstaff, T. Ferguson, J. Place, J. Ferguson. Front: R. Simpson, J. Vickers, T. Edwards, Dr Fielden, J.P. Shaw, G. Steele, T. Fletcher, John Bellis.

Shildon LNER Works Silver Band, 1937. The president was Wells Hood, works manager, and T. Collinson was the musical director. This photograph was probably taken in the railway institute building in Redworth Road.

Shildon Town Band, 1952. Show winners. Back row, left to right: J. Bell,
J. Dixon, ? Wren, T. Douthwaite, J. Thompson. Third row: I. Pearce,
F. Allinson, E. Bennett, L. Peacock, E. Lodge, A. Hardaker, B. Blackett. Second
row: T. Crook, G. Allinson, J. Allinson, J. Simpson, J. Etherington,
J. Whittaker. Front: B. Nicholson, B. Allan.

Back to more serious things. Shildon Works Home Guard in 1942. Over 70
men, very young and old. Are any of your relations here?

Sport in wartime, but with a serious purpose – 15th Durham Shooting
Competition. Cup presented by Lt Colonel N. Dewhurst OBE to No 9 Shildon
Works Company, January 1942. Back, left to right: Nat Peacock, Wilf Waton,
Anty Collins, Jack Coates, Willoughby Allen, Arthur Coates. Middle: Percy
Leng, Mr Cruddas (Works Manager), Capt Ware, Mr Ross (Asst Works
Manager), 2nd Lt Macquine. Front: unknown, Teddy Hall, Joe Wood, Bob
Sygrove.

Some family photographs of interest. First Holy Communion, 1971 at
St Thomas' RC Church, Byerley Road. Back, left to right: Craig Wilson, Keith
Thompson, Martin Peaker, Kevin Longstaff, Tracy Houghton, Susan Wilson,
Stephen Kaye, Eric McNaughton, Anthony Cook, Joseph Wade. Front: Christine
Mullen, ? Kaye, Sandra Mullen, Anthony Roe, Brian Wade. Priest, Father
Wilfrid Wright.

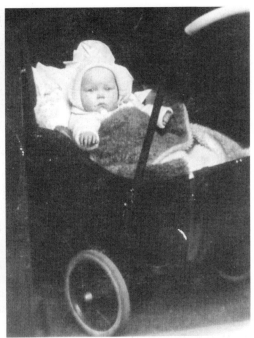

A Smithson postcard of Harry Thirkell, Charles Street, Shildon, in June 1902, at six weeks old. Harry worked at the wagon works as turner and machinist and then wheelwright for many years between and after the World Wars.

Over 30 years later in 1937. Anne Hodgson of Garbutt Street, Shildon. Note the change in clothing over the years.

Family and friends in the early 1920s. Back, left to right: Harriet Thirkell, Harry Thirkell, Edith Johnson (Harriet's sister), Ernie Johnson. Front: Jane (Jinny) Brown (Harriet's aunt), May Brown (cousin), Mary Hutchinson (Harriet's mother).

The next three photos are from the family album of Cliff Howe. First, on the right, is Robert Howe who was once a driver on the North Eastern Railway in the 1870s. He married Dorothy Skipsey whose father, John, was also an engine driver. In 1894 Robert was a hardware dealer in St John's Road, Shildon.

George Reynolds was a joiner who lived in Association Street, Shildon, from 1890. This family photo shows him extreme right with the child on his knee. His wife, Jane Ann, is extreme left. Her father, William Clement Walton, is third left back in bowler hat.

Above: The Local Board road
gang that George Reynolds
was part of. He is on the
extreme right with his tool
bag.

Right: T.H. White of Shildon
won prizes at various
carnivals during the Second
World War years
impersonating Hitler. Monies
collected were given to
charities.

A Chaplin family wedding photograph in Bolckow or Vaughan Street, Shildon, in 1907. Back, 4th left Mr Firbank (groom), 5th left Edith (bride), 6th left Margaret (mother). Front, left to right: John, unknown, Lewis, Jane, Kate, Frederick (father), Constance.

The Nunn family outside 15 Victoria Street, Shildon, in 1942. Left to right: Kathy, George, Hilda, Joyce, Martha Hubman (grandmother) and family friend Sid Johnson.

Right: Back to the 1920s. Edgar Clethero and his horse and cart outside the Primitive Methodist Chapel in St John's Road, New Shildon. The chapel was built in 1876.

Below: Edgar Clethero and his son Aubrey, with his first vehicle, a Morris, next to Dabble Duck Colliery site around 1928/9. Edgar hauled all sorts, from night soil to coal to furniture.

Left: Shildon, again in the 1920s. The Stones family outside their home in East View. Left to right: Elizabeth Freda, Jean and Thomas McDonald Stones.

Below: Poppy Day Appeal, late 1950s. Back, left to right: unknown, Doris Hall, Ida Wilson. Front: Kathleen Houghton, the Standard Bearer of the Women's Section of the Royal British Legion.

To finish off this section, some modern photographs from Heighington.
Heighington School, 1980, class J4. Back, left to right: Mr Dixon (head),
Richard Routledge, Craig Lyon, Adam Hall, Michael Lumb, Timothy Wright,
Paul Dodd, Ashley Platt, Mark Roland, Mr Gash (teacher). Second row: Philip
Fisk, Paul Haylett, Neal Denham, Karen Walton, Nichola Anderson, Elizabeth
Jackson, Jacqueline Armstrong, Paul Davidson, David White, Gerald Lee. Front
row: Rosemary Hindley, Katy Ward, Jane Neal, Sarah French, Adaline Sellers,
Karen Beadle, Julie Aire, Carol Trickett, Sarah Crowe.

A serious attempt in the year 2000 to determine how friendly the roads and
paths of the village were to disabled people. The local Women's Institute on
behalf of the Local Authority checking things out. Back, left to right: Carol
Gaunt, Judith Sellers, Janet Broomfield, David Sellers (some male brawn
required?). Front: Barbara Sellers, Angela Gooding, Joan Jackson.

Millennium Celebrations in Heighington in 2000. A representative group, left to right: Ian Gillies, Joe Henderson, Claire Moody, Helen Ferguson, Councillor Gerald Lee, Fred Pallister (oldest resident), Rebecca Henderson (youngest

school child), Matthew Hewitson, Rebecca Gault (at back), Edward Crawley, Jennifer Kirkley, Kate Dixon. There is another photograph showing all the residents of the village which appeared in the local press – too many people for a book of this size.

They've got a taste for celebrations in Heighington – and why not? The 2003 St George's Day celebrations on 23rd April, with from left: Hannah Garbutt, Ali Brown and Sarah Hemingway.

RAILWAYS, MINING & COMMERCE

A comic postcard showing the Shildon & Bishop Auckland Express, posted on 11th March 1908 from Evelyn to Mr Arthur Leng, 26 Lambton Street, Shildon. The writer says: 'Just thought I would send you a p/c seeing what a nice one it is. It looks very like you in the front with your girl, a nice smack for Shildon & Auckland isn't it. With best love.'

The opening of the following railway facilities in and around Shildon gives an idea of how the town was shaped and subsequently developed through its association with this form of transport:

27th September 1825: Witton Park to Stockton,
                      25 miles, and half-mile of Haggerleases Branch.
10th July 1827:   Black Boy Branch to Coundon, 1.5 miles.
1st May 1830:   Haggerleases Branch extended to Cockfield.
2nd October 1830:   Remainder of Haggerleases Branch, 5 miles total.
10th April 1842:   Shildon Tunnel opened, 1225 yards long.
8th November 1843:   Bishop Auckland to Crook.
13th September 1856: Shildon tunnel to West Auckland.

Immediately following 27th September 1825, the price of coal was cut by one-third, old pits began to expand and new ones were sunk. Within a radius of only two miles from the centre of Shildon, collieries were opened at Adelaide, Black Boy, Brusselton, Copy Crooks, Deanery, East Thickley, Eldon, Shildon Lodge, and South Durham by 1835, and all that coal mined and from further afield was transported through the town to the River Tees for export. From 100,000 tons of coal carried by the Stockton & Darlington Railway in 1828, there was an increase to 1,000,000 + tons in 1848, and over 2,500,000 tons in 1862. By that date there were 65 collieries in the Auckland Coalfield producing 4,700,000 tons annually. That industrial activity is recorded in the photographs and postcards to be seen in this section, along with the shops and other services that developed as a result of the significant population increases in the district.

A postcard from 90 years ago that highlights the key reasons for Shildon's development – coal and the railways. This is the north end of Prince of Wales Tunnel which opened on 10th April 1842 after three years of work at a cost of £100,000. The passenger train is heading for Bishop Auckland as it crosses the tunnel branch line which goes off to the right to West Auckland. The heavily-laden coal train on the left is waiting to complete marshalling the wagons before moving on. Off to the right of the photo is Adelaide Colliery, and to the left of the signal box, the branch line to Old Eldon and Eldon (South Durham) collieries.

Shildon Station about 95 years ago. The train, heading for Darlington, is stopping to pick up many passengers. Another train seems to be due at the north bound platform. To the left are the lines to the wagon works and the old Black Boy branch. The locomotive is No 1240 built in 1872 by the North Eastern Railway at North Road Works, Darlington. Christopher Churchman was the stationmaster in the first decade of the last century.

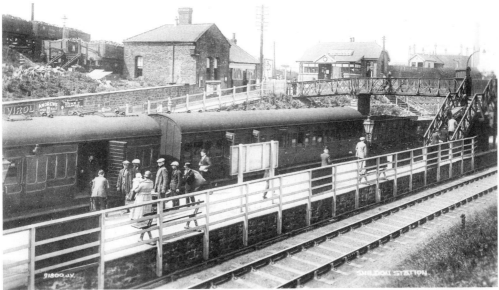

Shildon Station in the 1930s. Note the loaded coal wagons behind the building back left. On the platform the mother is waiting for the pram to be put on board. The advertisements for Virol, Andrews Liver Salts and Home & Colonial Teas are clear in this sharp print. P. Wrightson was the stationmaster in the '30s.

Another 1930s postcard, looking south from the footbridge. Again the station is busy as the train pulls in. Advertising at railway stations was big business in those days. This is the third station sited in Shildon, having been opened when the tunnel was completed in 1842.

Shildon Station at a later date, on 1st July 1965, as LMS class 4MT No 43057 locomotive pulls in with the 16.15 Heighington to Bishop Auckland train. Both the locomotive and buildings have seen better days.

Only 17 years ago, Shildon on 3rd August 1986 as diesel railcar No 143020/001 heads a Bishop Auckland to Saltburn train. The lines to Shildon Works have been taken up.

A steam special on 17th December 1994 as diesel locomotive No 47784 'Condover Hall' brings up the rear of the morning Santa steam special from Darlington to Stanhope. The steam locomotive heading the train is LMS class 2MT No 46441. The station has acquired the bus stop shelters common these days. All other station buildings have gone, and the sidings area to the left fenced off.

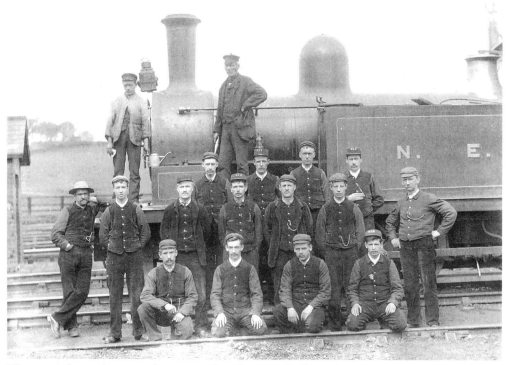

The next four pictures show people who worked on the railways at Shildon.
First, a group of North Eastern Railway workers in front of a class 1271
locomotive about 100 years ago.

Women cleaners on war work in the engine sheds at Shildon in 1918. They are
posed on NER locomotive class Q5 No 444. A Burns of Shildon photograph
published by Isaiah Dunn of King Edward Street.

Shildon Station staff in probably late North Eastern Railway days. The stationmaster listed in Kelly's 1925 Trade Directory was William H. Watson. Could that be him sitting between the two ladies?

A presentation to Mr J.H. Appleby, stationmaster, Shildon, on 30th November 1958, by G. Horner, relief stationmaster. Back left (standing on chairs): unknown, Billy Wilkinson, Sid Trueman, ? Izatt, Ernie Slack, Mary McInnely, ? Makinson, Marjorie Howes. Middle, short row: ? Pattinson, ? Rowling, Fred Gargett, unknown (eyes only), Dick Walker, Ted Grenfell, Cliff Howes. Front left: Joe Atkinson, Charlie Watson, Hyler Fairbank, G. Horner, Billy Blake, Frank Wood, G.H. Appleby, Jack Walker, Doris Whalen, Margaret Whalen, Mrs Trueman.

Heighington Station (originally called Aycliffe Lane) before the First World War when Moor Marshall was stationmaster. On the right where the man is standing is the original Stockton & Darlington Railway station platform where Locomotion No 1 was put on the rails in early September 1825. The locomotive pictured, No 910 of the 901 class, was built by Edward Fletcher at Gateshead NER Works in 1875. It is the only locomotive to appear at all three Stockton & Darlington Railway celebrations in 1875, 1925 and 1975. The message on the back to Mr R. Sowerby, 25 Elmfield Terrace, Darlington reads: 'Heighington. Dear Sir, in reply to yours of this morning, will be buried at 2.30 tomorrow Monday. J. Pearson.' Who was to be buried?

Heighington station about 40/50 years ago, looking towards Darlington. The platforms, staggered either side of the level crossing, were given the canopies in the Second World War years when the Royal Ordnance factory nearby was in full production and 12,000 workers used the railway daily.

Shildon Works branch on 7th May 1967 from the footbridge, facing east towards the station. On the left is Station Street and the Essoldo cinema.

Track lifting at the same location on 24th March 1985, after the works had closed. The Essoldo has also gone.

Shildon in earlier troubled times. In August 1911 there was a railway strike -
'Knox's strike' – which in Shildon took an unfortunate turn when the
stationmaster, a Mr Churchman, admonished striking engine drivers who
retaliated by chasing him, throwing stones at him, his house and passing trains
driven by 'blacklegs'. The outcome was the arrival of troops to keep order. This
postcard shows the soldiers on guard at the station.

Soldiers on the overbridge at the bottom of Dale Road. There is also a solitary
policeman.

Above:
Soldiers
resting at
the works,
though one
of them
seems to be
on guard.

Top right:
Soldiers on
look-out,
probably on
railway
premises at
the works.
There's also
three
civilians
there.

*Bottom
right*: A
soldier on
guard
adjacent to
the window-
damaged
signal box.
The strike
lasted for
eight days
from 17th
August.

To happier times. Stockton & Darlington Railway 150th celebrations at Shildon in 1975. First, a general view of the locomotives on display at the works on 29th August.

Getting ready for the grand procession on 31st August. First locomotive is LMS class 5 No 4767 named 'George Stephenson' a few days earlier.

LNER class A3 No 4472 'Flying Scotsman' pulling NER class No 910 in the procession.

LANDSALE.

FROM

SHILDON LODGE COLLIERY.

S. & D. R. CO'S WAY BILL.

14th day of June 1858

Proge. No.	Wagon. No.	Weight.	Description.	Destination and whom for
1	10964		Small	Eston Works
2	4500			do
3	10415			do
4	11457			do
5	1248	15		do
6	9866			do
7	10460			do
8	12963			do
9	9332		Uns.	Eston Depot
10	3088	15		do
11	142			do
12	11118			do
13	7072			Middlesbro
14	2041			do
15	3536			do
16	942			do
17	8392			do
18	6423			do
19	699			do
20	8666			do
21				
22				
23				

No. of Engine 141 Name of Engineman J.H. Barnes
Date May 13th Hour 8.55 am

These old Stockton & Darlington Railway documents illustrate the close relationship between coal mining and railways. The above weigh bill of 14th June 1858 identifies wagon loads of small coals to be delivered to Eston (steel) works and unsorted coal for Eston depot and Middlesbrough.

This illustration is from a log book of driver's hours on 13th May 1862 that shows that driver J.H. Barnes started work at 8.55am and was operating a coal train from Peases West (Crook) and Auckland Park collieries to Piercebridge and Barrow-in-Furness.

General Receipt.

Shildon Pass. Station

50000—16-10-76

May 3 1879

RECEIVED of the **North Eastern Railway** Company, the Sum of
One Pounds, one Shillings, and Nine Pence,
being amount due for Eight days Wages
Ending May the Third, Eighteen Hundred and
Seventynine

£ 1 = 1 = 9 Signature, J H Barnes

This illustration is a North Eastern Railway pay slip for £1 1s 9d for eight days wages ending 3rd May 1879 for J.H. Barnes. The above documents and many others were found by Jack Walker, Chief Clerk at Shildon, over 40 years ago in the rafters of the station buildings.

Two postcards of Shildon Lodge Colliery (Datton) in the early 1900s, showing winding engine building and chimney, and colliery offices on the right. This colliery – called Engine Pit then – was opened by Robert Surtees in 1830, and connected to the Stockton & Darlington Railway near Soho Works. Bolckow, Vaughan & Co worked this colliery from the 1850s to supply coal to their blast furnaces at Witton Park. The Brockwell seam, 5 ft 6 ins thick, was worked producing 800 tons daily, and later the Harvey, Busty and Low Main seams were worked. Bolckow & Vaughan also sunk the adjacent Furnace pit in 1864 – its name indicates the nature of that pit. Shildon Lodge was the biggest mine in Shildon and at its peak in 1914 employed 977 men. Different sources suggest the colliery closed in 1924 or 1926, but as a colliery called New Shildon Lodge operated from 1929-33, it is likely that the site itself did not completely close down till about 1937. A sports field covers much of the colliery site today.

Pit pony pulling a coal tub in 1906/7. It is decorated with awards won at the Bishop Auckland lifeboat appeal procession. Appeal processions were used to generate funds for hospitals and other services 100 years ago.

This Smithson of Shildon postcard of 1911 shows some workers from Shildon Lodge Colliery. Some of them may have lived in housing provided by Bolckow & Vaughan in streets named after the steel-makers on the opposite side of West Street (Road) to the colliery. Vaughan Street is still there today.

Shildon Colliery (or Dabble Duck – it was wet) was located at the junction of the Darlington-Bishop Auckland railway line through Shildon with the branch to the works (the old Brusselton incline branch), showing the engine house and winding gear. This colliery opened in 1866 and according to Whellen's 1894 Directory was worked by the Shildon Coal Co exploiting the Busty and Brockwell seams. The colliery employed 251 men in 1902, but by 1924 when it closed, only employed 30. It briefly re-opened, but was finally abandoned in 1927. The area is now an industrial estate. The locomotive is NER 1271 class No 1290 of 1875. It was withdrawn in 1915.

The shaft pump at Adelaide Colliery, Shildon. This 130 horse power pump was supplied by the Cleveland & Durham Power Co. The colliery was opened by Joseph Pease in 1830 and connected to the Black Boy branch of the Stockton & Darlington Railway, and later the Tunnel branch. According to Whellan, 1894, the Busty and Harvey seams were worked at depths of 150 and 126

fathoms respectively, the annual output was 150,000 tons, there were 139 coke ovens, and over 500 men were employed. However, the colliery closed in July 1924 with the loss of 400 jobs. The area has now been reclaimed for farming.

Eldon Colliery showing the chimneys and winding gear before the First World War. The colliery was part of a complex of pits opened from 1829 onwards which makes it difficult to confirm particular photographs even if they are captioned as pit names were swopped! However, Pease & Partners were running this colliery at the time of this postcard, and when war broke out in 1914 a total of 1,988 men were employed in three pits – Harry, Harvey and John Henry. By 1930 the workforce had reduced to 1,229, and in July 1932 the whole complex closed, leaving four men for the next 30 years on water pumping work.

A Smithson of Shildon postcard showing the coke ovens at Eldon Colliery. These ovens converted about 2,000 tons of coal into coke per week. In front there seems to be an expanse of water. According to Whellan, 1894, the colliery 'is much troubled with large feeders of water, and supplies the Dene Beck.'

Another Smithson card with the workers posed in front of the coke ovens at Eldon. At times about one quarter of the pit's total workforce was engaged on surface work, most of them in the coke works.

The local miners' lodge at Eldon parading outside the Royal Hotel, Close House before their trip to Durham for the Miners' Gala of 1913. The banner appears to be the old South Durham Lodge one of red and orange damask silk with a purple blue border. The Royal Hotel is still there today, but closed and boarded up.

A view from near the Black Boy incline of Eldon Colliery about 100 years ago. The terraced housing at the bottom of Eldon Bank can be seen, and off to the left the long rows of houses at Close House. It is said that the colliery owners, variously Pease & Partners, then Smithson, Samuel & Partners, then South Durham Coal Co, built over 250 houses for their workers in Eldon.

A much more modern photograph of miners going to the baths at Eldon Drift. These new pithead baths were opened by Sam Watson, Durham National Union of Mineworkers, on 11th November 1954, yet the drift closed in 1962.

In May 1990 when the area behind Shildon Hippodrome was being landscaped, this brick-lined tunnel, about 100 metres long which ran south eastwards towards Byerley Road, was uncovered by an earthmover. The next three photographs by Walter Nunn give an idea of the nature and size of the shaft, which was four metres wide and three tall. British Coal's response at the time was that it appeared to be the entrance to an early drift mine. However, another idea was that the tunnel was a means by which a Mr Bell, manager at Shildon Lodge Colliery, could get from his home to the pit without being seen by the workforce. Further research has suggested that the tunnel was a back-drift to Furnace Pit. A third of the way into the tunnel, the water table was reached. Old bottles were also found. Eventually, in June concrete blocks were used to block off the tunnel, and concrete then poured to cap it. After that it was landscaped.

Above: The shaft excavated.

Left: The size of the shaft in relation to the workman. Concrete blocks ready.

Concrete block wall completed, and concrete poured.

In Co-operative Street, Shildon, Thomas McDonald Stones, on left, with the Co-op horse and cart in about 1915. Mr Stones was a butcher.

The first recorded meeting of Bishop Auckland Industrial Co-operative & Provision Society Ltd took place on Saturday 25th February 1860 in the National Schoolroom, Church Street, Shildon, where it was agreed that each person should pay one shilling entrance fee and take up one £1 share, to be paid in instalments of one shilling per week. If Shildon was the birthplace of the Bishop Auckland Society, then Shildon was the seat of one of its keenest rivals – The Shildon and Neighbourhood Co-operative Corn Mill, Flour and Provision Society. That society had a large corn mill in Mill Street, New Shildon, and a store and manager's house in Church Street, but doesn't seem to have flourished. Eventually, on 17th November 1883 the Shildon Society Committee agreed to dissolve and wind up that society, and transfer the assets to the Bishop Auckland Society for £6,644 11s 2d. However, the corn mill didn't last long in new hands for on 3rd February 1888 it was destroyed by fire. Progress generally in Shildon was good in that sales doubled in the three years from takeover, premises enlarged in 1888, and additional property bought in 1892 and 1897. In addition, the Old and New Shildon Industrial Co-operative Butchers' Society amalgamated with its bigger neighbour in 1895. By 1910 – the Jubilee of the Bishop Auckland Society – there were the following premises in Shildon's Church Street: joiner's shop (where 1860 meeting was held), boots, groceries and drapery, butcher's and Co-operative hall. There was also 15 houses in Co-operative Street and a shop in Redworth Road, New Shildon. Today, nearly 100 years later, the Co-op is still in Shildon, in a supermarket at the junction of Church and Primitive Streets.

Shildon Boots.   Shildon Grocery.

Shildon Drapery.

New Shildon Premises.

Joiner's Shop, Shildon.

Shildon Butcher's Premises and Co-operative Hall.

C. Forbes, Beer Retailer. A postcard published by Isaiah Dunn, 20 Waverley Terrace. Compare this picture with the one at the bottom of page 105. It is the same location, same pose, same time probably. Two of a series by Dunn?

The Alma Inn; licensee Joseph Minnighan. In Kelly's Directory 1925, Joseph was listed as a beer retailer in Main Street. In 1938 he was at the Black Bull in Byerley Road; the Alma was being run by Fred Cockfield.

William Tait's licensed game shop in Shildon, showing rabbits hanging above (presumably) Mr Tait.

J. Pigg, grocer and provision merchants, Shildon. The Pigg family had premises at Alma Road and Queen Street as far back as 1906, and still had premises in Alma Road in 1938.

Walter Willson Ltd had premises in the north east 100 years ago. The two views here show the shop at Spencer Street, Eldon Lane, in 1930. In the picture, left to right: William Dixon, John Etherington and James Hannah. The premises were closed and boarded up in summer of 2003. The second picture shows the Walter Willson store in Station Street, New Shildon. Is that Henry Jones the manager in this inter-war photograph? The company also had a bigger shop in Church Street.

This photograph in Main Street shows the premises of Hackett & Baines, and also Christopher Smithson's photographic studios. Hackett and Baines have been in business for 100 years, starting off as general dealers, and now concentrating on specialist furniture. J.B. Smithson was a well-known photographer in Wensleydale at the end of the 19th century, and his son, Christopher, set up business in Shildon in about 1902. Many of the illustrations in this book were published by Smithson until he left the district in the early 1920s. Hackett & Baines took over Smithson's premises and doubled their shop frontage.

Right: Graham's bakers and confectioners in Shildon. Ronald M. Graham was at 26 Byerley Road in 1938 which is about the date of this photograph. Note the heavy advertising for Capstan Navy Cut and Will's Gold Flake cigarettes. A Chinese restaurant operates from the premises today.

Railways were the life-blood of Shildon, but other forms of transport had their place, as in this line-up of United buses in Church Street ready for an outing in 1928. The first four buses in the line-up belong to United's J class, with chassis built by the Associated Daimler Company and the bodies by United at their own works at Lowestoft.

	£	s	d
Moth frame-set. 22½" with gear fittings. Blue. No. 10240.	9-	0-	0.
1 pr. 27" wheels, Weinmann rims, Racelite hubs...............	4-	12-	6.
1 pr. J.B. Light speed tyres 38/4. 1 pr. J.B. tubes 13/10.....	2-	12-	2.
1 pr. rim tapes 2/-, 2 pr. track nuts 2/-.....................		4-	0.
1 pr. Dover mudguards 12/-, 1 Brampton 3/32 chain 10/3.........	1-	2-	3.
1 Brooks B.15 swallow saddle 35/-, 1 pr. Webb pedals 16/6.....	2-	11-	6.
Alloy handlebars, Maes 16/6, Presto handlebar stem £1.	1-	16-	6.
Benelux 5 speed tourist gear 50/-, freewheel 27/-.............	2-	17-	0.
1 pr. Weinmann brakes...	2-	1-	9.
Carradice 'Nelson' bag, 42/9, Brooks bag support 5/9..........	2-	8-	6.
Toe clips and straps...		9-	3.
Ever Ready front lamp complete 5/7, Starlite rear lamp 4/7....		10-	2.
Total:	**£30-**	**5-**	**7.**

Can you buy a bike today for anything like this price? Obviously not, but 46 years ago this itemised bill of £30 5s 7d from MacDonalds', 31 St John's Road, would buy you some bicycle!

SHILDON WORKS

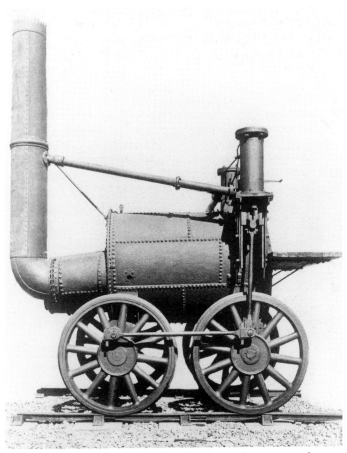

How it all started – Timothy Hackworth's original 'Sans Pareil' locomotive built at his own expense for the Rainhill Trials on the Liverpool & Manchester Railway in 1829.

When the Stockton & Darlington Railway opened in 1825 rudimentary workshops were provided for Timothy Hackworth, its superintendent, to maintain and repair the locomotives and wagons. He supervised a building containing a blacksmith's shop, joiner's shop, and an engine shed with space for two locomotives, and a payroll of 20 men. However, 1833 when Timothy Hackworth opened his Soho Works outside the front door of his home, and the Stockton & Darlington Railway erected 'extensive workshops at New Shildon for the building, as well as the repairing, of locomotive engines' (W.W. Tomlinson), is seen as the key date for railway works in the town. Both works built locomotives for the Stockton & Darlington, though after 1840 when Timothy Hackworth resigned as engineer to the railway to devote all of his time to his Soho works, he supplied locomotives for only a further two years. Many of his locomotives were supplied to other railways in the UK, and in 1836 he supplied the first locomotive to run in Russia. In 1855, five years after he died, the Soho Works were bought by the Stockton & Darlington Railway and used as an extension of the main works at New Shildon until 1883.

The main works saw much expansion between 1850 and 1860, with a new wagon repair shop, pattern shop, erecting shed, lathe shed and brass foundry, and new offices. Locomotives ceased to be built at Shildon in 1866 when the North Eastern Railway, which had amalgamated with the Stockton & Darlington in 1863, concentrated such building at nearby Darlington North Road Works. However, wagon building thrived and further works expansion occurred with the long engine repair shed (which originated in 1833, and finished up as a timber store at works closure in 1984) used for wagon repairs and in 1886 a blacksmith's shop built, along with a new forge three years later. By 1899 a new machine shop, sawmill, wagon building shop, paint shop and new offices for the staff and works manager had been constructed.

In 1936 the redundant engine shed was taken over and all wagon repairs concentrated there which allowed a re-organisation of the other shops on the site. After 1945, new shops were built for the construction and repair of steel wagons. A 1976 open day brochure stated that Shildon Works was the largest UK wagon works and could build 1,000 new wagons per year and repair 800 per week.

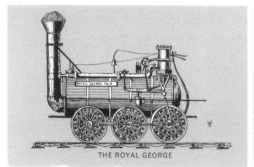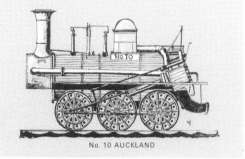

THE ROYAL GEORGE

No. 10 AUCKLAND

Two of Timothy Hackworth's locomotives for the Stockton & Darlington Railway. 'Royal George No 5' was built in 1827, and with six-coupled wheels had a significant increase in adhesion and power compared to its four-wheeled predecessors. Auckland 'Tory' class No 10 was built at Soho Works in 1839.

The west end of Timothy Hackworth's erecting shop at Shildon, built in 1833. This photograph from 80 years ago shows it in a semi-derelict condition, though it was not pulled down until 1966. It was situated behind Timothy Hackworth's house and workmen's cottages – now the Victorian and Railway Museum. In front and a few yards east of the museum, the Soho engine works of the same era is still intact and houses large exhibits.

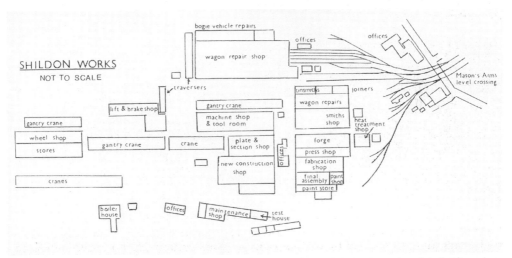

A plan of Shildon Wagon Works showing the facilities during the final 20 years of its existence. The 1976 brochure referred to previously, indicated that the works occupied an area of 44 acres, including a roofed workshop area of 13 acres, and employed 2,600 people.

Blacksmith's Shop. A Smithson postcard dating from around the First World War. This shop dates from 1886, and had forging and butt welding machines. Modern products included buffers, axle-guards and couplings.

The Machine Shop in 1920, where drilling, screwing, and production of dies and tools occurred. Notice the machines driven by belts. This is one of a series of posed photographs taken in the last years of existence of the North Eastern Railway.

Repair and Construction Shop, again in 1920. Many of these photographs are numbered – this being 117. It shows completed wooden wagons on the right and others at the stage of fitting steel body frame supports on the left. After the Second World War, new buildings were erected to cater for all-steel wagon construction.

The Sawmill, No 118 in 1920. This building was erected in 1897 when the North Eastern Railway considerably extended the works. Over the years the use of wood in wagons declined markedly, and this shop later became the plate and section shop shown on the plan on page 115.

Staff in the Timber Yard in 1920. Behind, in this photograph No 114, is the timber store which was built by the Stockton & Darlington Railway in 1833 as an engine repair shed.

Foremen and Clerks in this 1920 photograph, No 178. Why many of these photographs were taken in 1920 is unknown, but it was obvious that the railways in Great Britain were to be amalgamated into bigger units, so it could be that the North Eastern Railway was anticipating its demise and wished to record scenes for posterity.

Wagon Building Shop, No 128, in 1920. The script says: 'building of new wood wagons 20 ton – finished in April 1924.' The picture is thought to include 6th and 7th left: Bob and Anty Collins, and also two men with the surnames Patterson and Wardle.

The hand-written date on this photograph is 1907, and shows the Paint Shop staff ten years after the building was erected. Back: ? Lakeland, F. Best, H. Haw, E. Allison, T. Stabler, T. Connor, T. Rewell, W. Hodgson, unknown, N.W. Raine, T. Tweddle. Third row:

W. Haines, T. Fletcher, T. Cooper, A.F.W. Coates, G.H. Hewison, R. Rowntree, J. Abbot, F. Barker, J. Wood, unknown. Second row: F. Brown, H. Edgar, T.B. Pattinson, G. Rigg, R. Bunton, W. Smart, G.H. Brown, G.W. Kitching, M. Taylor, unknown, J. Johnson, T. Davison. Front: T. Hopps, E. Gardiner, J. Whitlock, W. Dodds, E. Vickers, J. Simpson, J. Briggs, J. Pattinson, J. Brown (foreman).

Another Shildon Works photograph, No 142, from November 1922 less than two months before the North Eastern Railway was amalgamated into the London & North Eastern Railway. From which working group are these men?

The Apprentices with their supervisor, 3rd left middle, on this photograph, No 140, of November 1922. Middle row, left to right: 7th Jack Yare. Front row, left: 1st Sydney Ebbage, 3rd ? Linsley, 7th Thomas Saunders.

Shildon Works in 1943. With a shortage of manpower due to the Second World War, the ladies, as they had done in the First World War, came to the rescue. About 100 of them are posed in front of the Black Bull public house. They worked on the railways, on the land, and about 15,000 at one time worked at the Royal Ordnance factory at Aycliffe.

Fitters and Mates at Shildon Works in 1954/55. They include: L. Brabbon, H. Close, C. Fishburn, T. Horan, A. Priestley, C. Smailes, T. Warne, A. Whitlock and Messrs Chester, Howard and Mawson. On 31st July 1954 there was a special opening of the wagon works by British Railways to celebrate the centenary of the North Eastern Railway. A booklet published at the time stated that 2,750 staff were employed who produced 9,500 new wagons and repaired 43,000 per year.

Shildon Works Office Staff 40/45 years ago. Back, left to right: N. Foster,
F. Gittens, R. Taylor, T. Rees, J. Ellenor, J. Watson, R. Woods, B. Scarff,
L. Lithgoe, F. Brownless, C. Rand, C. Allison, R. Tulley, L. Laetty, R. Clements,
E. Ewbank, A. Soakell. Middle: S. Watson, T. Bellis, J. Wild, W. Edwards,
E. Wright, T. Taylor, J. Hammond, H. Clarey, G. Hulatt, W. Robinson,
R. Cousins, unknown, D. Bulch, W. Cook, J. Edge, H. Manners, Joan Foster,
Rita Richardson. Front, sitting: Dorothy Kitchen, Margaret Nicholson,
S. Ebbage, June Bullyment (?), J. McMillan, F. Sowerby, A. Poole, ? Cooper,
? Lowery, W. Ibbotson, F. Mason, Penelope Clarkson, E. Wanless, unknown.

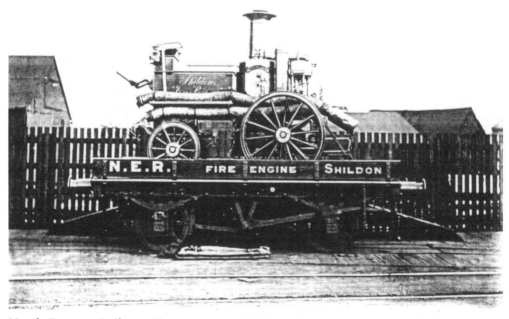

North Eastern Railway Fire Engine at Shildon Works in about 1920. Safety, and
a speedy response to all incidents were important.

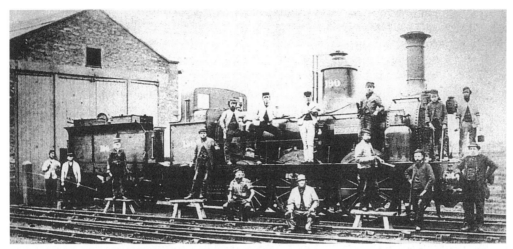

Some products from Shildon Works. Locomotives were manufactured from the opening of the Stockton & Darlington Railway in 1825 until about 1866 when building for the North Eastern Railway was concentrated at Darlington and Gateshead. This picture shows one of the last locomotives built at Shildon, in 1865 by William Bouch, No 190 Summer outside Soho Works paint shop in 1870.

A North Eastern Railway T30 ironstone wagon built in 1906.

Above: This view of the Wagon Repair Shop in 1961 shows wooden-bodied wagons and vans being repaired.

Left: Note the contrast between these modern photographs coming up and those from 80 years ago. A steel body being fitted on to its under-frame.

A general view of new wagon construction, which was running at 1,500 per year as late as 1980.

On 26th November 1980 there was a ceremony to celebrate the building of the 10,000th 'Merry-Go-Round' coal wagon. This photograph shows the normal work going on that day.

In April 1982, British Rail Engineering Ltd announced its intention to close Shildon Works in the following year. A temporary reprieve occurred, but the company argued that new wagon build orders for 1983 and into the foreseeable future did not justify keeping the works open. In addition, British Rail had started leasing wagons and allowing private firms to repair current stock. The result was inevitable, and closure occurred in 1984.

Shildon Shops

Imposing, forbidding, how great was your might
You spread across Shildon, formidable sight.
For one hundred years and fifty more,
Your wagons were constructed on every shop floor.
You employed nearly 3,000 personnel,
Labourers, staff and skilled craftsmen,
Who were dignified, loyal and proud.
When closure was mooted, their thoughts voiced aloud.
They – the Establishment – who would destroy our town,
Once hailed you as 'The jewel in the railway crown'.
Said these men, some fifth generation,
'We must meet, we must talk, let there be much oration,
Save our Shildon Shops we must',
Before the bulldozer grinds you into dust.
Marches were organised – your workforce went down,
Taking their anger to London town.
You had the support of one and all,
Could they see the writing on the wall?
Our efforts to save you were all in vain,
The Establishment did close you
Dear Shildon Shops
'Twas an act deemed quite insane.

Mary Wright

Another product from Shildon. A replica of Timothy Hackworth's locomotive 'Sans Pareil' had been built in 1980 for the 150th anniversary of the Liverpool & Manchester Railway. Here it is in 1995 giving steam rides on 18th June, Fathers' Day. It is heading towards the 1858 goods shed of the Stockton & Darlington Railway. To the right, behind the steel wagon, is the museum in Timothy Hackworth's old home.

Where the railways all started. A postcard showing four lads and a dog posing near Low West Thickley farm on the west side of the Brusselton incline of the Stockton & Darlington Railway. This is another Smithson of Shildon card from about 90-95 years ago. Note the track still in situ nearly 45 years after the incline had been made redundant by the opening of the tunnel branch from north Shildon to West Auckland. But what of the future?

Shildon will return to its railway roots when the new £8,000,000 railway village opens in 2004. The venture will combine the historic buildings and workshops of the Timothy Hackworth Museum with a 6,000 square metre out-station for the National Railway Museum. The site is expected to attract up to 50,000 visitors a year, including schools and large parties which will use it for educational purposes. Work started in September 2003 on a new building on the site of the old sidings west of the Darlington-Bishop Auckland passenger railway line. This building will house around 60 vehicles from the National Railway Collection, a shop, cafe, classrooms and conservation workshops. There will be modern, interactive interpretation of the exhibits, and in the workshops apprentices will be trained in the skills needed to restore and conserve railway vehicles. Timothy Hackworth Museum will be linked to the new building, and the space between will be used to incorporate interpretation and artwork. Continuing the railway theme, the proposed re-opening of the Weardale Railway from Bishop Auckland to Stanhope would complement and add to the attractions for rail enthusiasts to south west Durham – who could visit the Railway Village in Shildon and then board a preserved railway service up one of England's most beautiful dales. On a broader basis the Railway Village is expected to help not only the local tourist economy, but its general prosperity which will help the area look forward with confidence.

An artist's impression of the interior of the new building at Shildon Railway Village.

Back cover: The Sidings, Shildon, pre First World War, with an empty coal train heading towards the station. On the right is where the new building for the Railway Village is being erected.

The People's History

To receive a catalogue of our latest titles send a large SAE to:

The People's History
Suite 1
Byron House
Seaham Grange Business Park
Seaham
County Durham
SR7 0PY